Salt City Prayers

Salt City Prayers

ROBERT ALLAN HILL

RESOURCE *Publications* · Eugene, Oregon

SALT CITY PRAYERS

Resource Publications
An Imprint of Wipf and Stock Publishers
199 W. 8th Ave., Suite 3
Eugene, OR 97401

www.wipfandstock.com

PAPERBACK ISBN: 978-1-6667-8201-1
HARDCOVER ISBN: 978-1-6667-8202-8
EBOOK ISBN: 978-1-6667-8203-5

VERSION NUMBER 02/07/24

Portions of this book appeared previously in *Charles River: Essays and Meditations for Daily Reading* by Robert Allan Hill. United States: Resource Publications, 2015.

This book I happily dedicate to my dear, wonderful, musical wife, Janette Lee Pennock Hill. We met during high school in the neighborhood where these prayers were later offered. Now three children, three children-in-law, eight grandchildren, and ten pulpits later, her generous, loving spirit is the heart of and basis for our married life of 46 years.

Preface

The city of Syracuse, New York, is sometimes called by its nick-name "The Salt City," so earned because of its salt industry that prospered during much of the 19th century. Salt deposits across Central New York are thought to be a remnant of the Ice Age.

The Sunday morning prayers collected here were offered between 1985 and 1995 at Erwin United Methodist Church in Syracuse, New York.

But for the grace of God,
We would not be;
But for the grace of God,
We could not love;
But for the grace of God,
We should not speak.
But, by thy grace,
We live, and love, and speak;
By this grace, we are saved.
Alleluia.

Gracious God, loving and holy and just,
We lift our hearts in thanks and praise this morning.
We come to this sanctuary ready, again, to live as glad-hearted people.
With glad hearts, curious minds, and eager spirits, we offer ourselves in worship.
Bless us, we pray, by thy presence,
Which we invoke in the name of Jesus Christ,
our Lord.
Are we as ready as we should be to receive the gifts of Grace?
Have we been prepared, in these days, to notice the bountiful goodness by which Divine Love has touched us?
Do we need to confess a little slowness?
A little, occasional, lack of perception?
A shortness of spiritual breath?
A slight, or not-so-slight, disregard for what we have been given?
O Lord, as a people of glad heart,
We confess that we have not always been fully a people of open hands.
In these moments of silence,
Open us to a new rebirth of wonder.[1]

---

1. This prayer previously appeared in *Charles River: Essays and Meditations for Daily Reading.*

O Lord, our Lord,
How majestic is thy name, in all the earth.
The splendor of your creation resounds all about this day.
Teeming color, raucous sound, thrills of taste and touch—
The glory of this new day.
How majestic is thy name, O Lord.
Before you we lay the burden of the past week;
Before your gaze we unpack the satchel of our days past.
This week—its achievements, its sacrifices, its humor, its deadness,
its worry, its work,
Its height and breadth and depth—
We lay it all before you.
It is our hope to be in love with our brother and our neighbor.
We sit here today, hoping
That within these walls and among these souls,
We will find our salvation.
Teach us to live for one another, we pray.
We have neglected thy word and ordinances and now, in this sea-
son, we turn again to you.
Jesus Christ has claimed us as his own:
We are trying to live with that truth.
Defend us, we pray.

Dear Lord,

We offer a common prayer:

A prayer that our families, torn apart by abuse and distrust and anger and jealousy and unkindness, show kindness and pity to one another.

We offer a common prayer:

A prayer that our life decisions—about our callings, our use of time and our spending of money, about how we make not just a living but a life—will be illumined by grace and generosity.

We offer a common prayer:

That over time, and by hard experience, we may learn that the meaning of a word, a deed, an act is found not in the sentiment or feeling in which it was uttered or offered, but in what it does for others. Not in what we meant by it, but just in what it does to others.

We offer a common prayer:

A prayer that our grandfathers and mothers, in their age and infirmity, will receive care and kindness that accords with your warning to honor father and mother, so that our own days be long upon the earth.

We offer a common prayer:

A prayer that women, having been granted suffrage less than a hundred years ago—our grandmothers, mothers, sisters, daughters, granddaughters, all—will be spared any and all forms of harassment and abuse, verbal or physical, on college campuses, in homes and families, in offices and bars, in life and work.

And that they—long having suffered and now having suffrage—will
rise up, in our time, to be honored, revered, and compensated,
without reserve but with justice and mercy.

We offer a common prayer, finally:
A prayer not of this world, but of this world as a field of formation
for another;
A prayer not just for creation but for new creation, not just life but
eternal life;
Not just health but salvation, not just heart but soul;
Not just earth, but heaven.

"God of our weary years,
God of our silent tears,
Thou who hast brought us thus far on the way;
Thou who has by Thy might
Led us into the light,
Keep us forever in the path, we pray.
Lest, our feet stray from the places, Our God, where we met Thee,
Lest, our hearts, drunk with the wine of the world, we forget Thee;
Shadowed beneath Thy hand, may we forever stand,
True to our God, true to our native land."[2]

---

2. "Lift Every Voice and Sing" (1900) by James Weldon Johnson.

Dear God,

We come now to our weekly moment of common prayer.

You are invited to place yourself in a posture that supports and expresses the prayer of the heart—kneeling, standing, bowing, seated. We enter the prayer through the singing of our call to prayer: "Lead Me, Lord."

Gracious God, holy and just,
Thou from whom we come, and unto whom our spirits return,
Thou source of Wisdom, fount of Wisdom,
Wellspring of saving Wisdom:
Make of us, we pray, an addressable community,
That we might listen,
That we might hear,
That we might understand,
That we might listen, hear, and understand before we analyze or criticize.
Make of us, we pray, an addressable community.

Make of us, we pray, a benevolent community,
That we might polish our proclivity for the second thought, the second try, the second chance,
That we might expect to uncover a latent goodness, latent in ourselves and in others across this great, though troubled, globe,
That we might become good in ways that become the gospel.
Make of us, we pray, a benevolent community.

Make of us, we pray, a soulful community—
Alive to spirit, alive to love, alive to grace.

Take away from our souls all strain and stress.
Let us breathe again, breathe deeply, breathe the soulful breath of
life.
Make of us, we pray, a soulful community,
For we have gathered and bear witness to Jesus—our beacon, not
our boundary—who taught us to pray, saying . . .

Almighty God, our Heavenly Father—
Mysterious, anonymous, beyond all thought—
We rest before Thee this day,
Stopping in this sanctuary for just a few moments.
We come here hoping to see friends.
We come here expecting refreshment in familiar surroundings.
We come here aware, vaguely, of our need for Thee.
We come here in Christ's name.
Shake us free from the disappointment of our own blunders.
Stand by us to confirm our faith in you.
Cripple our self-indulgence, we pray.
Blind us to the blandishments of this world, we pray.
Regard us with that mercy which we cannot earn,
Yet can—and do—trust.
We have faith in thy love;
Give us confidence when faith falls short.

Father,
Forgive us whatever we have done, knowingly or not, that hurt others.

Forgive us our haughtiness,
Which makes us think that we can get along alone, by ourselves,
without others and without Thee.

Forgive us unkind words spoken in haste.
Remind us that to speak is good,
To think is better.

Forgive our foolishness, our neglect—
Of true love, and of the things that make for love.

Prepare us, whatever it takes, to partake of thy glory.

Remind us that, though we tarry here awhile,
Still we are going home.

For children, Lord, hear our prayer:
For hands that feed, for minds that teach, for arms that embrace,
For wise counsel, for careful guidance,
That our children might love these abundantly.

For those of us gathered here, Lord, hear our prayer:
That we might reach true adulthood as children of God.
Lord, hear our prayer.

In a season of change, may we embrace what lasts.
In a time of loss, may we hug the new.
In an era of decrease, may we find the unexpected.
In an epoch of debt, may we, sacrificially, endow the future.
In a day of disappointment, may we savor simple gifts.
In a month of worry, may we undress our anxiety.
In a year of decline, may we again see winter's gifts.
In an hour of depression, may we, with effort, accept kindness.
In a moment of fear, may we grasp the gift of faith.
In a morning of acedia, may we enter our prayer closet.
In an afternoon of besetting sin, may we recognize, humbly, our humanity.
In an evening of loneliness, may we experience graceful solitude.
As dusk comes, gracious God,
Help us walk in newness of life.[3]

---

3. This prayer previously appeared in *Charles River: Essays and Meditations for Daily Reading.*

Almighty and mysterious God:
With many different thoughts and words,
By many different actions,
We hunger for you.
Even when we claim to deny you,
We want to know your will.
We pray that, as a people,
We might find our way back to Thee.
Will you help us to exchange our national self-interest for a glimpse
of the justice of God?
We pray that, one by one,
We might learn to live—
Not absentmindedly,
Not driven by longings for pleasure,
Not harried, on the run, fighting an everlasting rearguard action,
Not carried away by self-satisfaction, or by lack of self-satisfaction,
Not fearful, not fearful, not fearful—
But faithfully,
Striving to live in thy sight.
Then shall we know Thee.
Come unto us as the rain, O God,
To strengthen us,
To give us good growth,
To feed us,
To fulfill the promise of our trust in Thee.

We pray to Thee.

Lift us by your Spirit, we ask.

Help us to lay aside all that depresses us or angers others.

Help us to lay aside all ill will, all cunning, all guile, all hypocrisy,
all envy.

Shut our mouths when we would speak ill of another.

Raise us to new life.

Help us to make camp around the fire of your love.

Give us the desire of newborn babes for the milk of sincerity, the
milk of your Word,

That we may grow thereby.

Lord, days past have we tasted your kindness,

But again we forget and go hungry. Feed us now, we ask.

Our hearts are tuned to the music of your church.

Kindle our imaginations too.

Show us escape routes, and underground railroads,
and Trojan horses,

And discoveries of the Spirit,

And new occasions for new duties,

That our heads might be more than hat racks,

And that, with our minds, we might love Thee.

For life and breath and this good earth,
We give Thee thanks, O Lord.
For people of kind hearts and generous spirits,
We give Thee thanks, O Lord.
For skillful craftsmen whose work praises Thee,
We give Thee thanks, O Lord.
For the Cross of Christ that reminds us of thy presence—
Even in the darkest hour—
We give Thee thanks, O Lord.
For the promise of heaven, for thy love beyond death,
We give Thee thanks, O Lord.
For the life in our communion of saints,
We give Thee thanks, O Lord.
The world around us changes with frightening speed:
Peace, where once there was cold war,
Tension and armament, where once there was order.
Nation rises against nation,
And we are more open to your word for us.
Random hurt has touched us, as a nation and a church.
A pleasant afternoon hour gives way to injury—
An evening of quiet, to a phone call with bad news.
A medical visit includes a disturbing portent for the future.
Our life has been touched by random hurt,
And we are open to your healing word.
The shadow of heaven has again fallen upon our patch of green
earth: to you we release another soul.
Even in Christ, O Lord,
We lack the tongue and the heart to face death,
So we are open to your word of grace.

In this season of returning,
As we return to home and school and church,
We are open to Thee.
Restore and rekindle our faith, we ask,
Through Christ, our Lord.

Dear Lord,
Out of all the confusion of this week,
We reach up our hearts to Thee.

Bowed and quiet, now,
Warmed and cheerful, here,
We stretch out our souls to Thee.

As your people, the sheep of your pasture, we turn again to Thee.
We pray to Thee claiming no big win, hiding from ourselves no sin,
big or small.

Promising no new resolution, yet.
Conceiving no masterpiece of our own.
Not trusting our own selves right now but praying to Thee.

O Holy God—
So far off and yet, somehow, so near,
Like light, like hope—
To Thee we do now pray.
Lord, hear our prayer.

We pray that paths of friendship will up between warring camps,
whether on the river Jordan or on Meadowbrook.

We pray that wise men and women will, in time, receive mantels of
authority, whether in Washington or in Cicero.

We pray that our willingness to criticize others will not overshadow
our reluctance to look at ourselves.

We pray that we will not fall in love with what hurts us—depression, addiction, cynicism, stoicism, eroticism.

We pray for a new rebirth of wonder at your Word.
We pray for clean winter quiet in our hearts.
We pray for our preacher, for our neighbor in need,
For children everywhere, for those constrained
to nursing homes,
For one who is sagging, for another who is bloated,
For another who is empty, for another who is full.

O Lord,
Thy silent presence bids us pray.
In thy presence, we are thankful and joyful and hopeful.

We bow before Thee.

Bowing our heads in reverence for Love, we make our common prayer.

In the stillness of this sanctuary, we are free to pray,

To bow before Thee,

To seek, again, a quiet center.

Speak to us, we ask.

Speak in silence, without words.

Speak of new life and love.

Speak in the quiet center, in the heart.

We bow before Thee.

Our bowing shows our intent to love Thee.

Help us to follow through, to carry through on our intention to love Thee.

We have meant to think kindly of those who criticize us behind our backs.

We have meant to look for good in those who find fault in us.

We have meant to live your Good News by speaking well of those who speak ill of us.

We have meant to smile at those who frown at us.

We have meant to forgive, firmly, those who have knowingly hurt us.

We have meant—by bearing quietly the injustice of this world and the ignorant libel of those with a worldly agenda—even to bear witness to Love.

We have meant, truly, to be your people.

And yet, dear Lord,

Now, in this luminescent quiet, realize the fragility of our intent.

It is not easy for us to walk out on this water.
It is not easy for us to stay awake in this garden.
It is not easy for us to stand out plainly and pay up personally.
We have meant to love our neighbor.
We have meant to love our enemy.
Lord, help us!
Help us, Lord, we pray!
Help us to follow through.

We thank you for the mothers of our church,
And for all those whose faithful mothering lives, today, in our bodies and in our worship.
We pray for the mothers of the new age:
In their activity, may still there be peace,
In their work, a sense of playful abandon,
In their exhaustion, a reminder of eternity.
In their anxiety over roles changed, rearranged, reversed, remade,
May still they cling to love as the reason for life.
We praise your holiness and love for those who have shared a maternal love with others' children—
Not only those who have children but also those who raise, teach, and love children are dear to Thee.
We pray for this nation as it struggles, over another decade, to settle the politics of the womb.
We pray for those in the springtime of life who are taking a new step toward love.
Thy life is within our souls, but our selfishness has not helped you.
Master us by your love, we ask.

This day we gather as baptized and believing Christian people, a people called Methodist,

Whose task it is to set forth a disciplined example of Christian service.

About us we see neighbors in need.

One is tripped up by her own self-concern.

Set her free!

Another is imprisoned by old and empty dreams that need replacing.

Set him free!

Another fears the future and dreads change.

Set her free!

Someone is lonely and growing bitter in her loneliness.

Set her free!

One cannot cut free from a web of frustrating relations.

Set him free!

Another has forgotten the promise of eternal life and so puts all his hope in this world.

Set him free!

Another does too much and will not rest.

Set her free!

Lord, let us soon sing to Thee a song of utter freedom, for "Our hearts are restless until they find their rest in Thee."[4]

4. *Confessions* (A.D. 397–400) by Augustine of Hippo.

Bless us, O Lord, we ask:
With the material of your grace,
With happiness,
With friends to understand,
With a church to absorb our extra pain,
With a love of learning,
With a hand stretched out to the stranger and traveler,
With tunes in our soul,
With a willingness to change,
With resolve to not overmuch fear what we cannot see,
With acceptance when we cannot change,
With forgiveness (for our own foibles first of all),
With a faithful memory,
With the material of your grace.
Bless us, we ask.

We do pray to Thee today in earnest, in serious reflection.
All our life is open to you:
Our good deeds,
Our burning hungers,
Our mistakes,
Our bad habits,
Our thinking.
There it is.
We lift our baggage to you.
Lord, hear our prayer.
Hear us, we beseech Thee, O Lord!

(Silence)

Today, we intercede for the needs of the world.
We pray that the hungry will be fed;
We pray that our nation will become just;
We pray that our children will stay clean;
We pray that our president will be healthy;
We pray that our bishop will be healthy;
We pray that love will grow here;
We pray that others will know Jesus through us;
We pray that we will not fear our enemies;
We pray that we will become more generous.
Hear us, we beseech Thee, O Lord.

(Silence)

We take the name of Jesus, the Outcast, and pray.

Eternal Spirit,
Before Thee all our words are inadequate—
Empty unless Thou fillest them,
Misdirected unless they be caught up by Thee.

Eternal Presence,
How odd it is that we so easily pass by the greatest gift of thy grace
to us.
We forget that you, and not we ourselves, have made us.
We forget that we are meant to be thy people, the sheep of thy
pasture.
Be we young or old, help us to wake each morning rejoicing at the
chance to praise thy name while yet we have breath.

Eternal Love,
We look about us, this day, and praise the loyalty of those who have
sacrificed on behalf of thy kingdom.
They have given up the freedom of solitude and joined together in
marriage;
Others have chosen to raise children in a Christian fashion, teach-
ing them to live simply so that others may simply live;
They have given hour after hour after hour to thy service in the
community.
All of them we pin with flowers and brush with kisses and praise,
this day,
For in them we see some loyalty to the Cross of Christ,
Which bids us dump out ourselves and drink deeply of others.

Eternal Christ,

Help us to realize, this day, that there are many sizes and shapes and kinds of families in this great land.

Help us to remember that Jesus said we must leave father and mother,

A rebuke to those who would make the family a kind of God in itself.

Help us to remember that the unnoticed and unthanked and un-mentioned and unremarked work of teaching children is what gives us the future.

Amen.

Heavenly Father,
In this season of light and darkness,
We bow our heads before Thee—
Our Maker, our Forgiver, our Sustainer—
And, for this moment, we forget our own needs.
Open us, we pray, to the cares of our brothers and sisters.
Remind us, in this season of celebration, that not all is joy.
Prepare us to handle the unexpected emotions and surprising encounters of the holidays.
Free us to take a moment of this Advent to do something for someone who can give us nothing in return.
We pray for families who have lost loved ones.
We pray for new families who celebrate their first Christmas together.
We pray for our young people—that they, through all the tinsel,
May yet catch a glimpse of thy pardoning love.
Do we know, Father, that we need to be forgiven?
Help us, at least, to know that we need forgiveness.
We pray for souls who stray from the gospel they once knew.
Bring them back, dear God.

How great Thou art.
These days past, we have been busy—
With ourselves,
Our homes, our health,
Our worries for loved ones,
Our uncertainty over the future in this cluttered world.
Lawns to mow,
Weddings to plan,
Driveways to seal,
Funerals to attend,
Irregular verbs to parse,
Letters to write,
Gardens to weed,
Books to read.
We have been tied up, lately, with our lives and our ways of love.
Now it is Sunday, and we stop to worship Thee.
We read, O Lord, that by your word we are made clean.
Speak to us now, and cleanse us.
We want to become better people, and a better nation, than we are.
We are eager to listen for, and to heed, your loving word.
We want to love our neighbor as ourselves.
Send thy love to cleanse us, like rain and red ground.
Clean us by your word.

Dear God,

Although you are too great and wonderful for our minds to comprehend,

Still we pray, this and every night.

We invoke your blessing for this church,

And for her many members and friends,

In the midst of uncertainty and worry.

We invoke your blessing to give us some certainty in the midst of uncertainty,

And some assurance in the midst of worry.

We invoke your blessing in the midst of these careless days,

That somehow, divinely,

We might be healed of our propensity to hurt and forget.

In the midst of greed and permissiveness,

We pray for a measure of discipline.

In the autumn of the year,

In the autumn of life,

Help us trust that there is splendor in loss, decay, and decline.

Help us to live splendid lives while the chill winds blow.

Make us colorful children—

Orange leaves in the November of Time.

We do invoke your blessing, Lord.

Lord,
My eyes have been, too much this week,
resting on things that perish.
My ears have been tuned to top-forty tunes
and not to the music of the spheres.
My lips have bent toward frowns instead of
smiling rays of love.
My voice has scolded when it could have sung;
My heart has wallowed in doubt and fear.
My mind has drifted to cheap entertainments
When I could have pondered the good and the true.
I want to follow Jesus, but I need help.
Take my hand; cleanse my heart.
Make me laugh with love, for all to see.

Dear God,
Thank you for everyone in this sanctuary,
For their reverence and for their faith.
We pray your blessing for us.
We have learned—some soon and some later—
That we need your love in every hour.
So, we have come to your sanctuary to worship.
Before you we remember our beloved nation, in its hour of planning and decision.
Guide us toward a gentler and kinder culture.
Deliver us from our neglect of the needy.
Take our minds off what we can do and put them on what we ought to do.
Give us the resolve to sacrifice for a better tomorrow.
We ask your help for our church.
Lord, we have hopes for our life together.
We hope to expand our ministry, to prepare for the future;
We hope to help children, the elderly, families, the poor.
We need your Spirit to empower us.
Are you running with us, Lord?
We thank you, God, for gracious people,
For humble and sensitive souls who make life fun.
Maybe you can, this week, bring out the best in all of us.

I am being driven forward
Into an unknown land.
The pass grows steeper—
The air, colder and sharper.
A wind from my known goal
Stirs the strings of expectation.
Come, let us adore him.

Dear God,

Our prayers go out:

For the brother in Christ who is feeling low, doubting his own worth and your own love,

Comfort him, we pray.

For the sister in Christ who is sick:

Comfort her, we pray.

For the brother who has lost his way,

Who has gone off to a far country and wasted himself:

Comfort him, we pray.

For the sister who worries and cannot seem to stop, though she knows and trusts Thee:

Comfort her, we pray.

For the brother who loses heart, who is easily discouraged because his hopes are so high:

Comfort him, we pray.

For the sister who loses herself in running and running and endless hectic activity:

Comfort her, we pray.

Dear God, holy and loving,
We pause in this evening hour to offer thanks and praise.
For the very gifts of life and faith, of community and work, of safe
space and gracious time, we are deeply thankful.

Bless our time together in this place, we pray.
For the daily chances to encourage one another, to give another
generation a place to grow in learning and virtue and piety, we are
truly thankful.

Bless our work together on this campus, we pray.
For the example of those honored tonight, whose steady service,
valued loyalty, and hard work we celebrate here, we are happy and
thankful.

Bless our life together across this great University, we pray.
Spirit of Life—Thou, our source of meaning and hope—
Before we break bread together, we pause to be thankful for bread
to break together, remembering those far and near who are in need.

"Now, on land and sea descending, brings the night its peace
profound. Let our vesper hymn be blending with the holy calm
around."[5]
We invoke thy blessing in this hour.
Amen.

---

5. "Now on land and sea descending" (1859) by Samuel Longfellow.
This prayer previously appeared in *Charles River: Essays and Meditations for Daily Reading.*

Heavenly Father,

In all our hope and in all our brokenness, we stand naked before you—

You, who knowest the inner workings of our minds and hearts.

We give thanks that in the name of Jesus we have caught a glimpse of you,

And that, in the grace of Christ, we have caught a glimpse of ourselves as we should, and might, and can, be.

We give thanks for blessed ones now dead,

Who have been directed toward Thee, and who have been defined (named!) by that inward inclination.

We give thanks:

For Quakers, who taught us to quake and tremble before the Word of God.

For Methodists, who taught us that self-discipline is a mark of discipleship.

For Baptists, who told us outright to choose between good and evil.

For Catholics, who have kept to the One Church in the hope that, one day, we will all be one again.

These saints would not listen patiently to lies, to gossip, to hurtful words.

They did not walk with evil, nor did they take delight in scoffing.

(How easy it is to scoff!)

No, they grew and bore fruit,

Like giant willow trees planted by streams of water.

To know the difference between good and evil, helpful and harmful, what builds up and what tears down—

This is our prayer.

For in the good we are, and become, familiar with Thee.

And the other?

You are not familiar with the other.
May thy grace be upon us!
The gift of the Cross of the Lord Jesus,
In whose name we pray.

Blessed Jesus,
At thy word we are gathered, all, to hear Thee.
Let our hearts and souls be stirred, now,
To seek and love and fear Thee.
Thou alone to God canst win us;
Thou can work all good within us.
We would be grateful, Lord—
As grateful as the child receiving his parents' affection;
As grateful as the spouses receiving each other on the day of their marriage;
As grateful as the elder receiving the whimsy and wisdom of old age—
Lord, we would be grateful.
We would be grateful, too, for what you call us to be and do.
We pray that our church will grow.
We pray that new people will find, through the witness of this congregation, a foretaste of thy love.
We pray that lives will be mended, souls surrendered, and spirits healed.
We pray that our congregation will grow.
We await—in the darkness and anger of our time—
We await a quickening of thy spirit.
Lord, we need Thee every hour.
We await the time foretold by the prophet Joel,
When our young men will dream dreams, and our old men will dream dreams—
When dreams will live—
When thy people will not fear.

Lord, we pray to be made grateful.
Lord, we pray that this church will grow.
We pray, too, for an endowment of dreams from on high.
In the name of the Father, and of the Son, and of the Holy Ghost.
Amen.

Before you we are silent, God.

*We are not fit to utter your name, so holy are you and so twisted we
are.*
In truth, we cannot bear the weight of your Presence.
To speak of you, and to you, surpasses our strength.

We are not angels but men,
Men of flesh and bone and twisted tongues.
Our help is in your name, Thou Maker of heaven and earth:
Tremendous, Awful, Mighty, Everlasting, Holy God.
In Christ, we come together.
In Christ, we hazard our prayer.
*In Christ, in him alone, we have confidence to pray as your
children.*

Lord, we beseech Thee: hear our prayer,
Hear our confession of sin.
We are ever not who we seem, or who we desire, to be.
*We waste our best selves, our most precious hours, our talents, our
money.*
Wasters all, we confess our sin.
*We make little room in our hearts for real outsiders; ours are closed
kitchens and dens.*
Saving ourselves, we lose our souls.
Loners all, we confess our sin.
*Daily we die a thousand fearful deaths, anticipating the worst, lack-
ing the faith we profess.*
Doubters all, we confess our sin.

Lord, have mercy on us.
Christ, have mercy on us.
Lord, have mercy on us.

Thanks and praise to Thee for allowing us this cleansing!
By love—yours—we are free to try again!
Undeserved acceptance we receive, even now!
Thanks and praise and honor and glory!
In Christ, we again feel free to taste another bittersweet day.
For this, we have come to worship.

Dear God, we thank you and praise you.
In prayer, we again come to faith.
In faith, we ask your intercession for those we see hurting and
alone:
For the young woman in the hospital;
For the mother, impatient and tired, feeling unappreciated and
inept;
For the worker whose job is on the line;
For those who are moving soon;
For the widow near death;
For the teacher who struggles;
For the teenager caught with cocaine;
For the husband whose wife may be ill;
For one who wonders if there is purpose in a quiet, retired life;
For the heart that has faith but lacks assurance;
For the ministers of the church;
For all your church, human and frail.
Intercede, we pray.
Thanks we give,
Confession we render,
Adoration we utter.
Lord, hear our prayer.

Eternal God, holy and loving,
For what we have in common, we give you thanks.
For this fragile planet, our common home.
For this great and troubled nation, our common project.
For this community, our common business.
For the chance together to speak and hear the truth,
Which moment by moment sets us free.
For the simple grace of this common meal, our fellowship today.
Eternal God, holy and loving,
Now, for what we have in common, we give you thanks.
Bless this food to our use, and us in thy service.[6]

6. Invocation for the Luncheon with Billy Graham at Dewitt Rotary, April 24, 1989.

I will give thanks with my whole heart, soul, mind, strength, with
everything that is in me,
Here in the congregation gathered to the people of God.
How great are thy works, dear Lord!
Those who study thy creation—
Biologists, chemists, physicists, Boy Scouts, Campfire Girls, the
elderly who take the time to stroll—
Take pleasure in thy works.
They remember and tell the wonder of thy creation,
A sign to us that Thou art gracious, merciful,
Forever mindful of your commitment, loyalty, and abiding care for
thy disturbed creatures.
Teach us, teach us,
Compel us to grasp hold of the Cross of Jesus:
There is your commitment, your loyalty, your abiding care.
Compel us to trust this Messiah,
Who knew the most hateful, the darkest things in life,
Who was raised up,
Who lives in the heart.
Jesus Christ!
Redemption!
A commitment forever!
The fear of the Lord is the beginning of wisdom.

Church,

Excitement and hope,

Triumph,

Serene joy of Eastertide.

Terror-torn world—

Nation and state in a time of decision—

Leaders—no judges in the land.

Wisdom of Solomon,

Compassion,

Vision of a common good,

Joy of spring, flowers, and sun.

Father, we are hounded by cares beyond our control.

These we lay before Thee:

The illness of a beloved partner,

A friend and wife suddenly hospitalized,

An unexpected success,

An engagement broken,

A project with little fruit,

A disagreement over something that really counts,

The discovery of a past deep hurt,

The return of a friend,

The courage to change one's mind,

A period of emptiness,

A business loss,

Worries about a drug-ridden country.

Our fears we lay at your feet.

In praise of Thee, we remember our joys!

Father, we are cut off—
From our neighbors, from our own best selves, and from Thee.
We walk alone.
We ache to have someone truly know us and enjoy us.
And, as we are cut off,
Much of what we say and do is distorted.
We say what we do not mean;
We do what we know to be hurtful.
Our anger spills over, and we disgrace ourselves and harm our friends.
We feel alone,
And so we despair.
We feel alone,
And so we become aggressive.
We feel alone,
And so we forget what it is to be happy.
We feel alone,
And so we want to control and intimidate others.
Gracious God!
Heal us, we pray!

Great art Thou, O Lord our God,
And fully to be praised, morning by morning.
We pray for thy blessing in this hour,
For thy gifts of confidence, certainty, and sureness
for the days to come.
Help us to receive, with confidence, the many surprising gifts em-
bedded in our personal lives.
Help us to notice the unexpected possibility, the new friend, the
unusual word, the strange connection.
Help us to see, with the confidence born of obedience, more than we
plan to see, to receive more than we expect to receive.
Teach us, as a church and as a congregation, to claim some cer-
tainty in the midst of uncertainty.
Teach us, we pray, the path we best should trod into the unforesee-
able future.
Teach us, rightly, to connect yesterday with tomorrow in the light of
thy certain love.
Shower with cool saving rain and moist power the leaders of this
world, with sureness to seek justice and peace.
Help those in the torn-up conflicts of our day to continue daily,
surely, to seek the promise of the Prince of Peace.
Kindle daily in the hearts of great leaders an even greater desire for
peace, with a sense that goodness and mercy shall surely follow.
Through Jesus Christ, our Lord.[7]

7. This prayer previously appeared in *Charles River: Essays and Meditations for Daily Reading.*

Our Heavenly Father,

*The joys of springtime, the simple pleasures of warmth and light
and growth, again make us joyful.*

Your morning has once more broken upon us,

Like the first morning in Eden's Garden,

And so we praise you with elation!

Our sin—our rapacity, our conceit, our slowness to sense the suffering of others—our sin deflates this spring of joy.

Forgive our doubt.

Forgive our ignorance.

Restore us, from death, to Christ our Savior.

Lord, Holy Spirit, our Life—

Draw us, again, into the fray.

Help us to do battle with the God of this world.

Today we pray for college graduates. Give them, we ask,

Maturity, patience, perspective, forbearance, character.

Give them personal maturity.

*Today we pray for those whose family lives are less than perfect—
that is, all of us.*

Remind us, Lord, of:

The squabbles in Jesus' family,

The jealousy of James,

The conflict with Mary,

The sayings about hatred of brother and sister.

Jesus knew family trouble. Help us to remember.

Today we pray for our leaders. Help them, through their votes, to preserve peace,

But to also promote a kind of justice that will be a foundation for lasting peace.

Father, in prayer today,

We lift up the joy of spring, the darkness of sin, and the power of your Spirit.

O Lord,

Our lives are circled by forces beyond our control.

Hear our prayer.

An uncertain future awaits our world, as nation wars with nation.

We pray for peace, for a forestalling of bloodshed,

For leaders with the wisdom that make peace.

The poor of the earth cry out for our help,

And we hear the cry, though a long way off.

May our ears be pricked that some peace will grow from a new justice in the world.

Life races past, and our days disappear before even we have held them close.

Abiding hurts clutter our minds and hearts;

A weariness befalls us.

Lord, we hear your call to us—

We hear your calling for us—

To follow Jesus.

Give us grace to pick up our cross and follow along.

Temper our anger, we pray.

Kindle our hope, we pray.

Inspire our outlook, we pray.

Quicken our imagination, we pray.

Open our mind, we pray.

Make us liberal folk, slow to judge, quick to give, eager to help,

Trusting in forgiveness that abounds beyond our willingness to believe it.

Heavenly Father,
This Easter morning, as we stand
Illumined and warmed by the resurrection light,
We pray thy blessing upon thy people.
Bless us with a desire to walk always hand in hand with Thee, day by day.
Bless us with an unquenchable outrage at the injustice in this world.
Empower us in our roles as citizens, family members, disciples of Jesus Christ,
To find strong, honest ways to help alleviate that injustice.
Bless us with the courage to give away that which we do not need,
And to see the connection between our prosperity and another's degradation.
Bless us with a single purpose in life—to love Thee—
So that our many little loyalties do not crowd out our one great loyalty:
To the truth that alone sets us free.
In Christ's name, we pray.

Father in heaven,
We have offended you.
We forget why we are here, and what truly lasts.
We are unwilling to love only Love.
We do not control our hungers,
We neglect to care for details,
We store up treasure on earth,
We are lazy.
We get angry at others when we have only ourselves to blame.
We thrive on flattery, whether true or false.
We are so busy with ourselves that we do not watch for you.

Yet, this morning, we are here.
Something warns us that Christ lives—
That Christ is yours, and we are his.
(If only we could live with this in our hearts!)
Where is faith?
Where are people who can trust enough to take some chances?
Where is hope?
Where are communities of people who have a good vision for the future?
Where is love?
Where does one go hungry so that another may eat?
Trust, desire, and sacrifice abide, these three;
We long to know them!

We are blind, deaf, mute, and disoriented.
Maybe we will stumble on faith, hope, and love—
But, God, if you lead us,

We will know them soon, and for sure;
For Thou, only, art holy—
Thou, only, art the Lord.
Amen.

Brothers and Sisters,
The Christ calls on you, now, to follow him.
He invites you to shun every form of evil,
To seek every kind of good,
And to worship God in public and in private.
He calls on you to consider the source of your life—
To consider its destiny—
To realize that this moment is later than you think.

The Christ calls on you to love your neighbor.
He shows you that you, like all men, are a sinner,
And he tells you that he can lead you out of even the deepest sin.
He warns you that, without the kind of love he inspires, this old world is without hope.
He reminds you that, though you tarry here awhile,
You are going home,
To a house made not with hands.

The Christ calls on you, now, to follow him,
To worship the Lord, thy God, with all thine heart and soul and mind and strength,
And to love thy neighbor as thyself.
He asks only this:
That in your heart you say, without falseness,
"Lord, I want to be a Christian."
Are you new to the faith?
Be baptized in this community, right soon.
Are you baptized, but at a distance from Christ?
Confirm your faith now.

Are you baptized and confirmed, but doubting?
Believe again, in the only person ever worthy of your belief:
The Crucified One.
Are you baptized and confirmed and believing, and in no special
need?
Mention it in prayer, right now.
Are you baptized and confirmed and believing, and in no special
need?
Then look about you, to those less fortunate,
And remember the words of the Lord—how he said,
"Just as you did it to one of the least of these brothers and sisters of
mine, you did it to me." [8]

The Lord Jesus Christ calls you to his banquet table.
Whether you hear the call for the first time or the fiftieth time,
Don't come late to the banquet.
The Christ calls on you, now, to follow him.

8. Matt 25:40, NRSV.

Heavenly Father,
We confess our sin before Thee.
We confess our misuse of privilege and possessions and positions.
We have used what we should love,
And we have loved what we should use.
We have used people; we have loved machines.
We have neglected thy Word for us as it is found in the Bible.
We have not pursued peace with all our might.
Forgive us, we pray,
Through Jesus Christ, our Lord.
Amen.

For our neighbor in need,
For our future,
For our church,
For peace in our time,
For grateful hearts,
For a willingness to risk,
For cleansing:
Give us the lessons of salvation,
To begin to float in faith,
To test intermediate strokes,
To achieve the rank of swimmer,
To be life savers, of and for others.

Dear God,

With praise for your power,

With thanks for your love,

With reverence for the mysterious grace in which we are held,

We kneel before Thee.

Fall upon our disordered lives, we pray.

Banish our tolerance of injustice;

Banish our tolerance of indifference;

Banish our undisciplined anxiety;

Banish our fear;

Banish our sin.

We confess that we have been foolish, faithless, heartless, ruthless.

Forgive us, we pray.

Raise us again to a disciplined life.

We remember before Thee the stark and horrible defects of this life:

Innocent victims,

Helpless neighbors,

Accidents,

The savage effects of illness, war, and loneliness.

Heal and restore, according to your will.

Heavenly Father!
Whatever is true,
Whatever is honorable,
Whatever is just,
Whatever is pure,
Whatever is lovely,
Whatever is gracious,
Whatever is excellent,
Whatever is praiseworthy,
Whatever is peace-worthy:
Center our minds on these things,
So we might know thy peace.
Renew us, dear God, in the Spirit of our minds.

Almighty God,
Lord of life and death,
Free us, we pray, from the things we wrongly fear.
Free us from superstition;
Free us from an unfaithful dread of death;
Free us from worry over the past.
We know that we cannot free ourselves—
Thou must save, and Thou alone.
Make us courageous people, we pray.
Free us from every destructive impulse,
Free us from greed and sloth;
Free us from envy of our brother;
Free us from overindulgence;
Free us from fear of the future.
Free us to serve Thee,
In Jesus' name.
Amen.

I invite you to seek the truth in our speaking and listening this morning.

We gather together to give thanks,

To hear the Word of God,

To remember that God, in this life we live before him, is Spirit.

They that worship him must worship in spirit and in truth.

Dear God,

Before your watchful gaze, we stop.

Within earshot of your attentive care, we bow down to worship.

Adorned in youth,

Adorned in maturity,

Adorned with knowledge,

Adorned with faith,

Adorned with wealth,

Adorned with struggle,

Adorned with piety,

Adorned with effort,

Adorned with commitment—

Before you, we bow down today.

We are naked before you.

Forgive us, we pray.

Will your Spirit stop our mouths, quicken our minds, tickle our eardrums?

Will we this week—attentive to your Spirit—wonder, cry, pray, hope, doubt, worry?

Help us listen for you, we pray,

To listen for you as we reckon with bitter and sweet memories,

To listen for you as we look backward on wrong choices,

To listen as we ponder tests yet to come,

To listen as we await the end of our days,

To listen as we risk, and work, for a new and better tomorrow.

Will we listen this week?

Everlasting and gracious God, our Father,
We praise thy name this day.
We sing thanksgiving for many blessings;
We shout for joy at the remembrance of Thee;
We jump and dance and celebrate thy goodness.
Lord, help the struggling hearts here present.
Lord, free us from fear of the future.
Lord, save us—when Satan afflicts us and we are hurt—from
bitterness.
Lord, keep us from the Evil One;
Keep our children safe, safe as can be.
Lord, we stand every hour in dire need of Thee,
But, in thy light and love, we begin to see.
Lord, grace those who are changing their lives,
So that the changes will be good ones.
Lord, care for our wills, so that we may learn
To be hard where we should be hard,
And soft where we should be soft,
And not the other way around.
Give us insight to see the frailty and the worth of thy church,
And to give our hearts, souls, minds, and strengths to its
upbuilding.
Help us to get up and try again,
Through Jesus Christ, our Lord.
Amen.

Almighty God,

Hidden from us, merciful to us, Judge over us:

Give us grace, we ask, to attend to the voice of truth, which calls to us.

We hear of the deaths of a million Arabs in Persia this past year: it is more than rumor of war.

We pause and are frightened.

Call us again to believe, to serve, to strive for peace.

We hear of misjudgment and bad faith and pride ruling from high places.

Who among us practices no cover-up?

Call us again to admit that we are more human than anything else.

Call us to appreciate, first, the good in others, and only then to judge the bad.

We hear from the words of Scripture a promise of heaven and a threat of hell.

In our dreams, in the late-night hours,

In the loneliness caused by the cage of our life,

We overhear the rumbling sentences of thy love—

And, if we are honest and alert, then we are afraid.

Call us to thyself,

That where Thou art, we might also be.

Gracious God,

Give us words and thoughts with which to offer Thee thanks for the abundance of gifts of creation,

Which the harvest shows us.

We thank Thee, Lord.

Much, if not all, has been safely gathered in,

Almost before the winter storms began.

You do provide for our wants to be supplied:

For harvest of grain and corn, for produce of milk,

For harvest in the great manufacture of our blessed land

(Rich in things, if not always so in soul),

For harvest of financial security, if we enjoy it.

And, with earnest prayers that the many who do not will soon be safe from want,

We give Thee highest thanks and praise,

And raise a joyful song of harvest home.

Gracious God, holy, loving—
Source of light and truth, goodness and beauty, honor and justice—
We bow, this day, to lift our hearts in praise and thanksgiving.
*We offer thanks for the excitement of discovery and the courage of
explorers:*
For those who have charted new lands,
For those who have found new cures,
For those who have produced awesome new energies,
*For those who have thought courageously with minds transformed
by grace.*
*For all in whose work we have glimpsed thine image, we sing thy
praise.*
O Lord, we lament, too,
*That amid exploration and discovery, we have made idols of our
own works.*
We have gloried in our own power to make and to destroy;
We have celebrated our own hazy goodness;
We have mistaken creature and creation for Creator.
*We have been too much impressed by human progress and too little
impressed by divine judgment.*
O Lord, we earnestly pray,
*Deliver us from the evil we have forged in our time, with our hands,
in our power, by our own hazy goodness—*
From the threat of thermonuclear holocaust,
From the threat of technological imprisonment,
From the threat of environmental collapse,
From the threat of comfort-induced amnesia—
And turn us, repentant, once more toward
The pure light of thy mercy.

Heavenly Father,
Hear our prayer today for those in need:
For the hungry and the war-torn,
For those facing difficult choices,
For families grieving in the hour of death,
For newlyweds now walking a new path,
For travelers,
For the ill.
Heavenly Father!
This is a rich land we inhabit:
Its skies are filled with the birds of the air;
Its waters teem with fish;
Its forests and fields bring forth abundance and shelter much life.
If through our praying we could make it so,
We ourselves would want to become—
To thy glory—
As rich as this land.
Rich in self-giving,
Rich in fullness of faith,
Rich in joy,
Rich in capacity for wonder.
Heavenly Father,
Turn us toward Thee in this hour.

Father,

We are thankful, today,

For the inspiration we feel here.

Here, we remember our faithful fathers and mothers;

Here we recall the days of our youth, when with keener minds and purer hearts we sang thy praise;

Here, we recharge by shaking the hand and feeling the closeness of our friends in Christ.

Here, we see the cross.

Father,

We come to worship, to open our hearts to Thee.

One comes, suffering in physical discomfort and the torment of the flesh.

Another comes, tired from a week of much motion but little progress.

Another comes, wondering if Thou art with us at all.

Another comes, worrying, with a difficult decision looming.

Another comes, frightened, for he has seen, spoken, and done evil.

Another comes, lost, needing to make a decision for Christ.

Pour out thy spirit upon us!

Forgive us,

And make us know that we are forgiven,

And help us to forgive others.

Amen.

O Lord,

Our Lord,

How majestic is thy name, in all the earth!

Open our ears to hear your voice!

In the rush of great waters,

We overhear your call.

In the clash of thunder,

We overhear your justice.

In the bustle of the city,

We overhear your voice.

In the quiet of the evening,

We overhear your mercy.

O Lord,

Quicken our devotion to Christ!

Enliven our attention to Thee!

Embolden our service to others!

Gracious God, our Heavenly Father,
By whose providential will are guided the nations of the earth:
Today, we thank Thee for blessings past and present and future.
How blest we have been, in days past,
With wise and careful leaders who, as did Joseph in Egypt,
Have kept us from famine and distress.
How blest we are, today,
With leaders who, as did Jacob on the river Jabbok,
Help us strive to meet human need and divine command.
How greatly we implore thy blessing for days to come!
Give us leaders who, as did Jeremiah,
Challenge us to commit ourselves to the common good.
Guide our peoples, we pray:
That with charity for all,
With malice toward none,
With firmness in the right—
As Thou dost give us to see the right—
We may pursue the cause of liberty,
Ever prizing that freedom for which Christ has set us free.

Heavenly Father!
Come and rule in our hearts this day!
We come here to worship Thee,
And to wonder what Thou would have us
Do,
Think,
Say,
Be.
We gather,
Some with burning questions,
Some with painful choices before us,
Some with illness close at hand,
Some captured by fear—
Fear of death,
Fear of life,
Fear of failure,
Fear brought on by boredom and loneliness.
Set us free—to serve Thee, and to have done with lesser things!
Great unknown of suffering,
Make us sensitive, imaginative truth-tellers,
So as not to trample on art and heart.
Give us strength to give up that which must be given up
Before we may come home.
May thy love be shed abroad in our hearts,
for all the world to see.

Eternal Spirit,
Rest, we pray, upon the souls here gathered.
Our birth and our growth, our decay and our death
Lie beneath the gusts of your movement.
We are aware of our ultimate and absolute dependence.
Hear our prayer for the penultimate needs of the world.
Some there are who struggle to breathe the very breath of life—
Quicken them, we pray.
Some there are who gasp to take in the oxygen of liberty—
Suffocating, as they are, in broken relationships, in imprisonment,
in slavery, in exile.
Some there are who lack even a touch of the Spirit of eternity—
They are material agents in a material world.
Make us all, rather, agents of your love and destiny.
Some there are who choke on the misdeeds of others—
Grant them recovery, we pray.
Hear our prayers for the penultimate needs of this life:
May we live as if surrounded by,
Buoyed by,
Swept along by
Your Spirit.
In Christ's name.

Dear Lord,

Accept, this day, our offering of praise and thanksgiving.

We gather as a congregation of thy people:

In our weakness and in our strength, we pause before Thee.

Father, you have cursed our blindness, and still we have not seen;

You have decried our passivity and pacifism, and still we have not striven;

You have judged our deafness, and still we have not heard.

Give us grace to turn around and to stop our pollution.

Make us graceful to watch for thy love—

Lord, hear our prayer.

Make us graceful to fight for thy love—

Lord, hear our prayer.

Make us graceful to pray for thy love—

Lord, hear our prayer.

For, without Thee,

We are fouler than anything and worse than nothing.

Save us from our sin, we pray.

Heavenly Father:
Who can stand in your presence?
Which one of us is fit for your everlasting love?
To the searching, searing light of your care,
We dare, this morning, to present ourselves.
How shall we deny your illumination of the darkened rooms in our souls?
We are dependent on your forgiveness, love, guidance, help.
Without you we are helpless, like sheep without a shepherd.
Tend to our waywardness, we pray.

Today, we pray for those of your flock who, across this land, are graduating from school, from college, from one living to another.
In their hearts and hands lies some of the destiny of this world.
In their hour of triumph, give them the sources of future love:

Give them gratitude. Give them compunction.
Make them grateful to have been spared (those that were)
The physical misery and crushing effects of hunger, of war, of home-lessness, of poverty.

Make them aware, too, we pray, of the contribution every personal selfishness makes to the ongoing horror of this world.
May they have courage as well as intellect,
Moral accountability as well as bank accounts,
A desire to please God as well as a desire to please parent, spouse, and self.

We pray for this new generation of graduates pushed forward, in
cap and gown, on the relentless wave of time,
Into an earthly tomorrow, but toward a heavenly home.

And may the love in this congregation also catch fire
From the gratitude and compunction left smoldering for us in the
Cross of Christ.

Heavenly Father,
Gracious God,
Our Creator, our Redeemer, our Preserver,
May we draw nearer to Thee, this evening,
In our thinking,
In our speaking,
In our listening.
May we see Thee in things that please and refresh us;
May we hear Thee behind, and beyond, things that perplex us.
May we draw nearer to Thee, this evening.
With thanks for nourishment, fellowship, and relaxation,
We pray thy blessing on our time together.
Forgive us all our sins, for Christ's sake.
Amen.

Heavenly Father,
What thanks we give Thee, for the gift of another day!
For the chance to live faithfully, to be thy children,
To purge ourselves of impatience, jealousy, doubt, and of anger, still harbored against our neighbor and against Thee.
We struggle with our lower nature.
We ask for willpower to cast off the tempting advice of the flesh.
We have begun with the spirit; we would not end with the flesh.
We look for peace of mind, Lord,
And sometimes we don't find it—
Past tragedy haunts us like a ghost.
Help us to know that the past is forgiven!
We look for peace in our heart of hearts:
Grant us such peace.
We pray that the fragile peace of this world will be maintained.
Before Thee, we remember the trouble in the South Atlantic, in the Middle East, behind the Iron Curtain:
Give us strong, wise, compassionate, humble leaders,
Who will keep a just and lasting peace.
We pray for our brothers and sisters, French and English, in Quebec,
That they might find a fair compromise.
With all the saints alive and dead, in heaven and on earth,
We pray in thy name, O Lord.
Amen.

Father!
We have called out to you;
We have watched our children grow and become adults;
We have worried and hoped and cried and laughed
Over what they did and did not do.
We have been angry.
Still we are puzzled by some things;
Still we are unsure of some things;
Still we worry about our children.
Your love has dawned in our hearts.
We see a little better in the light of the cross—
The light of Jesus Raised, shining out from the dark cross—
We see a little better.
We want our children to be happy, but more, we want them to
know Thee:
To know thy care,
To know thy demand for resolute living,
Thy demand for obedience.
We want them to have a calling in life;
We want them to have direction, to have work,
And to follow their fellow men, and Thee.
Pull us free from our vices,
Even the ones we most enjoy!
Mostly, we would pass on to our young that which we believe.
We know whom we can trust:
Father!

This prayer opened with the recitation of Psalm 100.

Eternal God,
Shrouded in Mercy,
We invoke your blessing this evening.
Before you we lay our common project: the work of this Boy Scout Council.
We pray your guidance for its leaders, your care for its supporters, your providence for its future.
Father, we pray especially for our young men:
Give them brave hearts for the hard choices ahead;
Give them reverent hearts so that, as they grow in stature, they may also grow in their knowledge and love of Thee.
Tonight, we are anxious for the well-being of our nation and our countrymen.
We pray for our leaders:
Give them the wisdom and patience that these difficult days require.
O Lord, as we break bread together,
May our fellowship and our conversation be acceptable in thy sight—
O Thou, who are our rock and our redeemer.
Amen.[9]

9. Invocation for the Boy Scouts of America Boy Power Dinner with speaker Howard Cosell, Syracuse Carrier Dome, April 15, 1986.

Lord,
Speak to us, we pray.
Speak in a voice clear and strong
To remind us, through our willful deafness,
Of thy love, thy will, thy judgment.
Speak in somber tones
To brace us against all that makes life cheap and shallow and
hateful.
Speak in winsome, soft sounds
To bear us up when we are weak.
Speak in silence,
Speak thy peace,
Speak to us of thy salvation,
Speak in shouts, and a cry of command,
To call us to obedience and belief.
Lord!
Speak to us, we pray!
Through Christ, our Lord.
Amen.

Good morning.
In this hour, we are asked to think about
The will of God.
In this hour, we are invited to remember
God's care for his creation.
In this hour, we are lifted up by
The power of the spirit of God in our midst!

Dear Sister God,
You held me at my birth.
You sang my name, were glad to see my face.
You are my sky, my shining sun.
And in your love, there is always room
To be and grow, yet find a home:
A settled place.

Heavenly Father,
We remember the crucifixion of thy Anointed One,
And we gladly gather to celebrate his resurrection,
Praying that this raising of Jesus will truly mean, for us,
Forgiveness of what is past,
Even that we might forgive ourselves,
And so lighten our daily burden.
Praying that this raising of Jesus will truly mean, for us,
Acceptance of what is present,
For we fear the anxious spirit that forever belittles what is present
in favor of what has gone by, or what is to come.
Help us to accept what the present has to offer.
Praying that this raising of Jesus will truly mean, for us,
That the future is open, thine,
Made in the image of thy Son.
Beyond death Thou art guiding us;
In this life Thou art guiding us.
May Jesus' resurrection mean, for us,
A forgiven past,
An accepted present,
An open future.
In Christ's name.
Amen.

This is a time of meditation.
It is a time to measure the past,
To recall past goodness.
It is a time to ponder the future,
To estimate the distance and the drama ahead.
It is an hour, and a moment, of refreshment.
The light shines in the darkness.
"For I am convinced that neither death, nor life,
Nor angels, nor rulers,
Nor things present, nor things to come,
Nor powers, nor height, nor depth,
Nor anything else in all creation,
Will be able to separate us from the love of God
in Christ Jesus our Lord." [10]
This is a time of meditation.

10. Rom 8:38–39, NRSV.

For the need of our world,
That it may be filled by thy grace
And by human obedience,
Lord, hear our prayer.
For peace,
Lord, hear our prayer.
For patience among rich and poor,
Lord, hear our prayer.
For wisdom,
Lord, hear our prayer.
For giving,
Lord, hear our prayer.
For healing: body, mind, spirit,
Lord, hear our prayer.
For courage,
Lord, hear our prayer.
For prosperity,
Lord, hear our prayer.
For fellow feeling and community love,
Lord, hear our prayer.
For young learning,
Lord, hear our prayer.
For the lonely,
Lord, hear our prayer.

In hours of quiet,
In wintertime,
We turn again to you,
Almighty and everlasting Spirit of Forgiveness.
In hours of quiet,
We remember what we need.
In quiet hours,
We await deliverance at hand.
Change our gloom to gaiety!
Shame us for our listless boredom!
Excite us about life and love!
Break the shackles of fear!
(Why do we fear such little things?)
And set us free, to hope again!
In hours of quiet, in the winter—
While nature pauses and kneels to pray and remember Thee,
While the field lies fallow,
While the river lies quiet in ice,
While the air hangs cold and crystal and clean with winter,
While all nature pauses to pray—
May we, too, have courage
To listen,
To lie fallow,
To lie quiet in ice,
To hear Thee.
Restore us!
Fit us again for spiritual combat!
Place us again on the battle line!
Draft us into the army of forgiveness!

O Lord, our Lord,

How majestic is thy name, in all the earth.

Hear our prayers as we lay them before Thee,

For in our hands no price we bring;

Simply to the cross we cling.

*For order and purpose in a world of turmoil, the cacophonous
chaos of our days—*

Lord, hear our prayer.

For moments to rest,

In which to lie down angry, disheartened, and tired,

But to rise up, again walking with Thee—

Lord, hear our prayer.

For protection, when others act like wolves and we feel sheepish,

*And for restraint, when history makes us as wolves and we are
hungry—*

Lord, hear our prayer.

For the courage to face, and trust, what most frightens us,

Be it new life, death at hand, our work—even Thee—

Lord, hear our prayer.

For the grace to forgive ourselves, following your example—

Lord, hear our prayer.

For the gift of mirth that keeps us sober—

Lord, hear our prayer.

Heavenly Father,

We wait on Thee in this hour,

Seeing ourselves, and our world, in a new light—

A Christmas light—

A light of different force and direction,

One that measures us against the birth of a poor child in a dark
cave in a foreign land.

We pray for what we need,

Yet knowing that Thou knowest our every thought

Even before it is formed into words on our lips.

Give us the vision of Joseph,

Who, by the help of an angel,

Saw in Mary's condition more than betrayal and shame,

But in it sensed thy will,

And so did not fear to take a wife already pregnant—

Did not fear but trusted in thy presence and purpose.

We lack a vision of how to live together on this earth in trust and
not fear.

Help us to see beyond the balance of power,

Beyond the glorification of achievement,

Beyond the wisdom of men and nations

(Which is pure folly)

To a vision of life together on earth

As it is, already, in heaven.

We need the vision of Joseph.

Give us the constancy of Mary,

Who knew Thee, not in the sphere of success but on the field of
failure and low estate;
Who bore Thee in the foulness of a manger,
And there saw the exaltation of the poor, those of low degree.
Mary had the power to see things through.
This we lack,
For we want immediate, visible, tangible proof of thy ways and
purpose,
And immediate return on our investment in Thee
(So we say).
We haven't the patience to be with Thee in the manger.
Remind us that haste is always of the devil,
And put some steel in our spines,
And give us the patience and long-suffering of the mother of God.
We need the constancy of Mary.

We need again to hope in Jesus, for we have wandered off,
Hoping in so many other things;
Placing our trust—like gamblers at a roulette wheel—
On things that do not pay off;
Confiding in the ruler of this world—
The prince of darkness—
Who proffers us comfort but not security,
Who tempts us to exchange our greatest hopes and dreams for
poverty of spirit.
We need again to hope in Jesus, and not in our own prowess.

This Christmas,
We ask for vision, constancy, and hope.
Amen.

Lord God,

Return to us in Jesus, the Chosen One.

You alone are our shepherd, our guide;

With Thee we shall never want for another chance for new life when the old path has become cluttered and unpassable.

We thank you when you make us, force us, to lie down and rest,

To be refreshed by an inkling of your presence,

To be restored by the knowledge that we are creatures, created to serve you.

Sometimes we do right—

And that feels good, to know that we have done right,

That we have served the cause of justice.

It is an act of worship, to do what is right before Thee,

And it truly pains us that we are not more often capable of doing right.

Sometimes we end up in the valley of darkness,

And there is a mighty anger in us when we see

Unrelieved sickness,

Sudden, unfair tragedy,

Corrosion brought on by fearful, selfish living—

Then, there is anger in us.

We give thanks that in this darkness,

Your light is on us,

Your song is in our hearts.

You are great to comfort us.

Sometimes we are trapped, hemmed in by enemies—

Then do we learn to savor thy gifts:

Food for the body, anointing oil for the soul.

Surely goodness and mercy shall follow us all the days of our lives,

And we shall dwell in the house of the Lord, forever.

Our Heavenly Father,
How happy we are to be in your presence this holy day.
This place is a sanctuary for us;
These brothers and sisters in the faith are our real family.
This time of quiet and thought, of confession and pardon,
Helps us with our life before Thee.
It is good to be here.
Our hearts are full, today.
This world is very much with us:
Concern for captors and captives around the globe,
Concern for the leaders of nations,
Concern for the great city of Syracuse in this election time,
Concern for our University, its Chapel, and the gospel ministry it is meant to promote.
Concern for those who once were two and now are one,
Who walk alone—
That is, alone with you.
Concern for those who mourn, those to whom you promise comfort.
Concern for the lost and troubled in our neighborhood.
Concern for the young woman, somewhere nearby, who has left her newborn on the doorstep of our parish.
Concern for those who, like Lot's wife, cannot resist the temptation to dwell on the past.
Concern for these days of September, and for our calling in this time.
Our hearts are full today;
Many are our concerns.
Are they your concerns, as well?

This prayer began with the telling of the Parable of the Good Samaritan, Luke 10:25–37.

Heavenly Father!
How thankful are we,
For life and breath and sense to speak of Thee.
We have no ability for Christian life, except what Thou givest us
when, through thy spirit, Thou touchest us.
We gather, here and now, to be reminded that, in the hardest spots,
we are asked to witness to Christ.
When we are angry—and have good cause to be,
May we live Christ.
When we are tired—and rest seems a ways off,
May we live Christ.
When the body hungers—after what does not nourish,
May we live Christ.
When we are green with envy—and there is no help for it,
May we live Christ.
When our buttons pop with pride—and we are justly proud,
May we live Christ.
When the joys and comforts of this world consume us,
May we live Christ.
We gather to be reminded that our neighbors lie bleeding on the
roadside, and we can help.
Heavenly Father!
Help us to live as Christians this week.

God of peace,
Grant us peace as thy power for honest love.
We have isolated ourselves from that peace.
In hours of rancor, in days of worry, in nights of foreboding,
We have closed our ears to thy command of peace.
Still: Thou art our refuge and our strength,
Our fortitude and our hiding place,
Our reason to rise in the morning,
The closure from darkness of the past,
The cleansing of our warlike ways.
Grant us peace, we pray:
Peace in our hearts as we start another day,
Peace to share with those we meet,
Peace in our work, peace down deep—
To help us take on tough tasks, anxious people, uncertain hours—
Peace through the time of sickness and of trial.
God of peace,
Grant us thy peace as a power for honest love.

Eternal God,
Give us pause, we pray, at the utterance of thy name!

O Thou, who art as close as our next breath and yet as far from us
as the morning and evening stars:
To Thee we raise our voices and lift our hearts.
Before Thee we lay down our burdens of guilt and hate and fear
and distrust—
And they are heavy burdens.
Will you teach us, again, to take upon ourselves the yoke that is
easy and the burden that is light?
Will you make of us a joyful people?
Will you make of us a happy people?
Will you make of us a prayerful people?

We pray for those of our company who struggle with the darkness
of life.
For one, the path ahead has become impassable, and another road
must be sought.
Teach us thy presence.
For another, the solitary journey becomes less like solitude and
more like loneliness.
Teach us thy presence.
For another, the frightful acrimony of family conflict overwhelms
and destroys.
Teach us thy peace.
For another, the need to succeed, at any price, warps mind and
heart.
Teach us thy peace.

For another, the weakness of the flesh—its frailty, its decay, its tyr-
anny—produces madness.

Teach us thy patience.

For another, the shadows lengthen along the valley of death.

Teach us thy patience.

Amen.

Heavenly Father,
Our hearts sing to Thee this day,
Amidst all the craziness of our earthly days.
In the midst of walls to paint and cars to repair,
And dishes to wash and children to raise,
And parents to care for and trips to take,
And meetings to attend and diapers to change,
And medicine to give and medicine to take,
And taxes to pay and promises to keep—
In the midst of our broken, hectic, lonely and confusing days,
Our hearts sing to Thee.
O Lord, how majestic is thy name, in all the earth!
We pray that the crisis of our times will usher in a time of peace for
our children:
A time of patience and forgiveness,
A time of cooperation,
A time of forbearance and self-control,
A time when one of your children will lay down their life for
another,
A time of peace.

Gracious God,

Our Heavenly Father,

Source of life, Maker of all things, sole Judge of all people:

To Thee we raise our hearts.

We ask your blessing for the holiday season.

As the days darken, spur us to shine with the light of love and truth.

As the pace quickens, gentle us to pause, pray, listen, and help.

As our joy abounds, point us toward joyless spots, shivering souls,
addicted brothers, abusive behavior,

And help us share with others.

As we bask in the comforts of life,

Hold before us the Cross of Christ,

In whose service we find

Meaning for life,

Light in darkness,

Joy in December,

And words of prayer.

Dear God,

We pause in prayer to place before you all the past year has taught.

Our learning from this year we present to you.

We bundle together what we have known and the ways we have grown:

In tasks partly completed,

In challenges met,

In losses unexpected and foreseen,

In spurts of creative energy,

In disappointments,

In surprises,

In changed relationships.

All this past experience we give over to your care and keeping.

Together, we seek your blessing for what is yet to be.

We seek your blessings of imagination and insight for the learning in the year to come:

For keen eyes, that we may sense unexpected opportunity;

For faithful ears, that we may hear a call to speak Truth;

For steady obedience to Christ Jesus—his teaching, his healing, his church, his spirit;

For curiosity, that we may discern the odd joys embedded in trials.

O Lord, we pray: make, of all that will come toward us,

A pattern of meaningful learning and growth.

For all that has been, we offer Thanks;

For all that will be, we say Yes.

Through the same Jesus Christ, our Lord.

Amen.[11]

---

11. This prayer previously appeared in *Charles River: Essays and Meditations for Daily Reading.*

Father,

Help us to confess before Thee our awkwardness, waywardness,
selfishness, and sin.

While the word of the world is therapy, let our word be forgiveness;

While the word of the world is analysis, let our word be pardon.

Help us to confess our sin;

Help us to face our past.

Wash us today, we pray.

Send over us the rush of mighty waters;

Send over us the cold pure water of thy love;

Send over us the dew and moisture of thy lavish grace,

That we might confess—

That we might have the courage to confess—

That we might have the courage and insight to confess our sin.

Prepare us to meet the truth of thy Word, in all its rigor, harshness,
wonder, and power.

Prepare us for thy presence, we pray.

We confess our sin,

Through Jesus Christ, our Lord.

Amen.

Father,

We pray:

Be with the sick, the tired, the lost, the feeble;

Be with the hungry and the homeless;

Be with the spenders and the spent;

Be with the troubled and those of restless heart.

Give them, once refreshed, the courage to again take up their struggle.

Be with the healthy,

That they might know of, and pity, and relieve, the sick.

Be with the strong,

That they might offer their strength to the weak.

Be with the well fed,

That they might share their bounty with the undernourished.

Be with those of our church and community now hospitalized, shut in, cut off from the natural flow of life.

Be especially with those persons whom we each name, in our hearts, as needful of your presence and peace.

In Christ's name, we pray.

Our Father,

We listen today, in this hour, for your words of challenge and of help.

Touch us as we listen and wait, as we worry and help.

Teach us to pray.

Help us as we rise each morning to meet the day,

And shower and shave and comb and press,

And bathe ourselves in a moment of silence before Thee.

Help us, as we pause to be fed each morning—noon—night—to ask to be fed, also, by grace.

Help us, when night has fallen, and we cover ourselves in the warmth and comfort of bed clothes,

To also cover ourselves in a simple remembrance of thy love.

Teach us that "weeping may linger for the night,

But joy comes with the morning."[12]

Teach us that we, too,

Can sing some songs in the night.

---

12. Ps 30:5, NRSV.

Eternal, mysterious, holy God,
In these moments of quiet, and in this place of sanctuary,
We praise you.
Our bodies praise you standing, bowing, kneeling, still.
Our voices praise you in song and word.
Our minds praise you in thought and questioning.
Our spirits praise you because we gather together.
Laying our relationships before you,
We confess our sin:
We have spoken ill of our neighbor;
We have misused our freedom;
We have doubted in unfaithful ways;
We have kept silence from cowardice;
We have tuned out the cries of the truly needy;
We have settled for slipshod judgments;
We have been overgrown by the cares of this world.
Forgive us, we pray.
Gird us up, we pray.
Ennoble our minds and set us on paths of truth and peace.
Lift us up, we pray.
Inspire our hearts for a time, that we again might learn the joy of
giving.
Hold us up, we pray, to be authentic witnesses that others can trust
and understand.
Hold us together, we pray.
Give us keen feeling for the hurt of another,
Eager longing to help another,
Wise judgment to avoid harming another,
This day, this week, this season.

Heavenly Father,
We give thanks for this meal,
For the strength it gives our bodies.
Teach us to always remember with thanksgiving
Our dependence on nature, on our fellow humans, and on Thee.
So we pray, in the name of Jesus of Nazareth,
Whose courage and compassion are our unfailing inspiration.

Heavenly Father!
Thou hast caused us to hear the good news of saving grace,
Brought to us on the cross and by the empty tomb.
We stand in awe and perplexity, in wonder and disbelief,
Before a love that shatters even the barrier of death.
How can these things be?
And how can we be worthy of them?
We have sinned.
We have thought ourselves to be the center of the universe;
We have scoffed at our utter need of Thee.
We have treated our neighbors, even our loved ones, with callousness.
We are unfit for heaven,
And we make the earth unfit, as well.

Heavenly Father!
What wondrous love is this, that speaks to us from the cross?
Grant us grace to live in an abiding memory of thy care,
So we may be ever ready to care for those about us.
Make us mindful, we pray, of those who suffer:
Those who are physically ill,
Those who are mentally tormented,
Those who are hopelessly poor,
Those who have lost loved ones,
Those who are caught in the guilt of sin.
Make us mindful of their suffering,
So that we may take from them the bitterest sting of suffering:
The fear that it must be endured in loneliness.
Lord, suffering we can bear, if only we have fellowship;

It is in loneliness that suffering becomes unbearable.
Give us grace to relieve the bitterest sting for those who suffer.
In these brilliant autumn days,
We stand aghast before the wonder of thy creation,
And murmur, once again, "How great Thou art."
May that greatness keep us humble.
Through Jesus Christ, our Lord.
Amen.

Most gracious Heavenly Father,
Who has safely brought us to the beginning of this day,
Defend us, this day, by thy power.
Grant that we fall into no sin, and run into no danger,
And that all our doings may be ordered by thy governance,
So that we do, always, what is acceptable in thy sight.
Through Jesus Christ, our Lord.
Amen.[13]

13. This prayer has been slightly adapted from "Morning Prayer," found in the Church of England's *Book of Common Prayer* (1662).

A Prayer for Maundy Thursday.

O Lord,
Amid the changes of this season and of our common life, we bow
before Thee.
We believe that heaven and earth are full of your glory,
Yet our prayers are not always so frequent or spirited or confident
as they should be.
Is it our pride of heart?
Is it our poverty of imagination?
Is it our neglect of discipline?
Is it our concern for the treasures of this world?
Lord, teach us to pray as the Apostle would have us do:
To pray without ceasing.
On this evening, Lord, as we recall betrayal and suffering, teach us,
we ask, a lively sympathy for others.
Tonight, we pray for those of our number—part of our commu-
nion—who are laden with burdens of the flesh:
We pray for Robert, Stella, Rhoda, Harriet, Ida, Florence, Julia,
Lena, Beulah, Ernestine, Marion, Gerald, Lewis, Lenore, Ken,
Emma, Gladys, Louise, Ruth, Vera, Laura, and so many others
whom we name in our hearts.
Already, we trust, art Thou present to bring peace—though not as
the world gives.
In prayer, and through sympathy,
Teach us obedience, we pray.
Through Christ, our Lord.
Amen.

Heavenly Father,
With the sounds of this past week still ringing in our ears,
We pause before Thee.
With the dust of this past week still clinging to our feet,
We pause before Thee.
With the memory of this past week still fresh in our mind,
We pause before Thee.
Lord, hear our prayer:
All that has been, between this sabbath and the last, we offer to
you—
The discoveries,
The taste of new food;
The handshake of a new friend;
The losses, of neighbors familiar and unfamiliar;
The surprises, the startling return of an old acquaintance;
The unexpected news of victory or defeat;
The births and beginnings and baptisms;
The decisions and delays and deaths.
All that has been:
We give to you,
We lay before you,
We offer to you,
O eternal Holy Spirit.

Living God,

Our Father, Guide, Judge, King, Maker, Hope, Eternal Rest:

We give Thee thanks that Thou hast placed this world under attack—

That Thou hast invaded it in the person of thy Son,

Our Lord Jesus Christ,

To whom we turn, in our hour of prayer and praise, awaiting news of his kingdom.

What news have you for us, Lord?

What news of thy kingdom?

What is the report?

Where and how shall we await the coming of thy kingdom?

Where and how can we be of service to Thee?

Teach us, Lord, for we are unworthy servants—

Never to one thing constant,

Undisciplined, uninspired, ungrateful, unkempt, unhappy, undecided.

Where and how shall we serve thy kingdom as Thou putest our world under attack?

Help us to put away all shameful acts.

Father,

Inspire in us, again, the desire to live only for Thee:

To strive only for thy kingdom,

To worry only over those things that matter to Thee,

To forget our foolish and selfish ways,

To love Thee and our neighbor,

And to love Thee by loving our neighbor.

Father, free us from fears:

Fear that our job is not important enough,

Our country, not pure enough.

Remind us that any work is great when greatly pursued;

That any home where love and joy and peace are found is rich enough, and surpassing;

That true religion is simple, and simply of the heart,

And is found in heartfelt service to others;

And that a country is, and stands, only as it collectively seeks thy will.

Father, put our minds on the future.

Help us to think of heaven, and of heaven on earth.

Give us great-hearted people in our land,

Who are willing to dream of a time when selfishness and greed and hunger and need have disappeared,

And the earth is full of the glory of heaven

As the waters cover the sea.

Put our minds on the other future, too.

Force us to have sure hope of heaven.

Help us to live each moment in the conviction that we shall dwell in the resurrection with Thee.

Help us to think of being raised from the dead;
Help us to believe in Jesus Christ, who is the resurrection and the life.

Father, into thy hands
We commit the care of our loved ones who are ill:
Heal them! Comfort them! Give them faith and courage!
Spare them unnecessary suffering!

Father,
Forgive us our sins,
Through Jesus Christ, our Lord,
By whom and with whom, in the unity of the Holy Spirit,
All glory and honor be unto Thee.
Amen.

Lord, help us to trust you:
When we face the unknown that always frightens us,
When we recall with regret a time gone by,
When we are tired,
When we are tempted to put a lesser loyalty before our faith.
Lord, help us to look to you and not just at other men, princes
though they be.
With concern, we look about us and see our many brothers and
sisters who are out of work,
Who live with the great sorrows that unemployment brings,
And yet we feel we can do so little.
We pray for enough prosperity that even the poorest will have shel-
ter and food and clothing and heat,
And some hope for the future.
Some of our young people have gone on to college, to the military, to
work away from home—
Now we miss them, and pray that they will do us proud, and that
they will find ways to serve Thee with gladness.
Instill in us thy spirit, we pray.
Fill us with love and joy and peace and patience and kindness and
goodness and faithfulness and gentleness and self-control.
Amen.

Almighty and everlasting God,
Our Creator, Redeemer, and Sustainer,
Who by thy love has made us, and through thy love has kept us,
and in thy love would make us perfect:
Lord, we find it hard to be grateful.
Our waywardness and pride forever obscure and confuse our place
before Thee.

We find it hard to be truly grateful,
For, to be so, we must give up many of our claims to fame.
No longer can we say, "Look what I have done."
No longer dare we mutter, "Lord, you could have done better."
No longer can we boast, "See what I have accomplished."
No longer can we cheer, "This, we have done well."

We find it truly hard to be grateful,
For to be so, we must remind ourselves that we are creatures—
sheep—in another's pasture,
Dependent on Thee in life and death.
We have what Thou givest,
We are what Thou makest,
We do what Thou wouldst permit.
Hard as it is for us to remember,
We are thy people, the sheep of thy pasture.
Thy life is within our souls, but our selfishness hath hindered Thee.

Heavenly Father,
This harvest before our eyes recalls yet another harvest.
We sense about us a hidden harvest of the spirit.
For that which this hidden harvest bears, we thank Thee, Lord:
For loving communities that care for their young and old and sick,
For joyful souls who preserve the frolic of youth into adulthood,
For men and women of peace, who warn of the consequences of fear and isolation,
For patient teachers,
For kind employers,
For good parents,
For faithful churchgoers,
For gentle, gentle husbands and wives who show us how to be gentle people,
For those who exercise self-control.
For this great, hidden harvest of fruit of the spirit,
We give Thee thanks and praise,
And raise the song of harvest home.
Even so, Lord, quickly come—
Raise the final harvest home—
Lord of harvest, grant that we
Wholesome grain, and pure, may be.

Father,
Today we pray, urgently, for deliverance from evil.
About us, rancor abounds.
This season of holidays and of lights
Surprises us with unexpected emotions.
One is anger;
Another is vengeance;
A third is hatred;
Another is remorse.
Amid the turkey and the dressing, the tinsel and holly,
There is seething rancor.
Deliver us from the evil of family life,
We pray.

We are drawn up short.
We lay before Thee:
Aloneness,
Dismay at the waste in human lives,
Guilt that we don't do more with what we have,
Prayers of intercession.
We are drawn to Thee still.
Turn us inside out.
Our trust is in Thee.
Lord, we tarry here awhile,
But we are going home.

In this hour,

We stand before a God who has lifted up many generations and has seen them pass away.

We come before a God whose love has already seized the generations to come.

We give thanks for our place in the march of generations.

So "Let the sea roar, and all that fills it;

The world and those who live in it.

Let the floods clap their hands;

Let the hills sing together for joy at the presence of the Lord,

For he is coming to judge the earth.

He will judge the world with righteousness,

And the peoples with equity." [14]

Give us grace, dear Lord,

To allow those about us to be free.

Have we conquered this land only to forget

That for freedom, Christ has set us free?

Some about allow us freedom:

How great they are!

Some of our neighbors will permit us to be what we will be without trying to control us.

For freedom, Christ has set us free;

Let us not, then, return to slavery.

Keep us from enslaving others.

Let us live and let live,

Free to be as Thou would lead us.

14. Ps 98:7–9, NRSV.

Gracious God, our Maker,
Holy Lord, our Helper amid troubles,
O Thou Mystery, hidden Power of pardon:
Together we pray for those among thy children who are in need.
For the elderly in Bosnia who, in mere months, have seen the work
of a lifetime destroyed, and have watched the whole world look past
their pain;
For children in America today;
For all who have seen evil, and done wrong;
For saints who grieve—lonely, hungering for one now gone—without complaint;
For young people disappointed;
For ministers of your gospel;
For one struggling to face the past, and the future, in faith;
For new ventures begun in hope;
For hatchets buried, corners turned, dust shaken, leaves overturned;
For our church—its people, its ministry, its "second-mile" giving, its worship life;
For our friends;
We pray.
Amen.

Heavenly Father,
We cling to Thee in this hour.
Help us, we pray,
To lay ourselves before Thee,
To know our lives in thy sight,
To see our lives—the shortness of our lives—
To remember that our time is the space of a few handbreadths,
To remember our lives as thy gift to us,
To hope that, in our time, we may come
To a relationship with Thee through thy Son, Jesus Christ.
Help us to remember that the gift Thou hast given us includes a task, as well:
That we are here not without purpose, not without work, not without reason for being,
But that we are called to obedience.
Here, we need help.
We miss the narrow way;
We need to be led back.
When we are on the way, we find it difficult not to turn around.
We find it easier to wall ourselves up, to shut ourselves off.
We know that we would, on the narrow way, have real communion.
We find it easier not to grow.
We prefer what is familiar, even if the familiar hurts us.

Heavenly Father,
In the speaking and hearing of thy name alone do we expect to find
Freedom, peace, deliverance,
From the pettiness that clouds our minds and warps our will and
discourages us.
Straightaway do we expect deliverance
From the infrastructure of material gods with which we and our
children live.
We give thanks for talented people near and far,
Who, through their abilities, give us hope
That the massive problems which face us also have solutions.
For scientists, engineers, builders, architects, planners, and all
whom they direct,
We give thanks.
Out of the depths of our hearts do we cry to Thee, dear God,
Hoping for a cleansing, a redirection,
And a sense of new life
In Jesus' name.

God of love and God of power,
Our origin and our destination,
Our help in time of trouble,
Our Guide through struggle,
Source of our best hope and highest dream,
We give Thee thanks for this:
Another day, for this further opportunity to know Thee,
And to do—even in this late hour—thy will.
Send thy speedy blessing on those who hunger and thirst for Thee.
Almighty God,
We pray that Thou wouldst interrupt our lives and thoughts,
causing us to gaze upward, to recognize our need of Thee.
Heavenly Father, deny us when we lean toward selfishness.
Eternal Spirit, announce yourself, enter into our lives;
Change our patterns of thinking and doing.
Amen.

Dear God,

With the pain and the glory of this past week trailing at our feet, we enter your house to pray.

By design or habit or fear or longing, we have been carried to this place, and now we pause before Thee.

God of life beyond death,

God of forgiveness beyond sin,

God who raises the dead and frees the prisoner:

To Thee we lift our hearts.

For reminders of your law, we give thanks.

For the harsh teaching of experience—in which the law we break breaks us—

We offer some thanks.

No other God but Thee do we seek;

No human art finally fills us.

Help us to not pray in vain or miss the chance for worship.

Instruct us, we pray, in how to love our neighbor, honor elders, choose life, be true, be fair, be honest, be happy.

O Lord, into our homes this week

The long shadow of absence and emptiness has, somehow, stretched.

We are shaken: by the illness of friends, the mistakes of loved ones,

By hurt inflicted and endured, plans gone awry, chances missed.

All our sorrow we now wrap up and leave at your altar.

Thank you, dear God,

That by thy grace, joy, too, has warmed our homes:

Birth,

Problems faced and solved,

Reconciliation,

Healing,

New Life.

All our joys, too,

We commend to Thee as spiritual offerings.

Lord, teach us to pray as we ought and need.

We do ask in Jesus' name.

Amen.

Dear Lord and Father of mankind,
Forgive our foolish ways.
Cast out our sin, and enter in.
Be born in us today.
As the days grow shorter and the nights longer,
Help us to not only look but to listen for Thee.
Help us to hear, where our sight fades into darkness.
Help us to hear the overtones of thy presence.
Help us to listen for Thee.

Some of us come to worship, today, truly looking and longing for
Thee.
We sense that we, alone, fall short.
Dress us up in an assurance of thy care:
Our undue striving will stop,
Our constant straining will cease,
Our fear of our own real selves will melt before the words "Thou
art."
Will we make the journey to Bethlehem?
Will we be ready for Christmas?
In all our preparation, will we notice the invasion of One who bids
we be prepared for him himself?
Prepared for not only his birthday, but all days?
Help us to hear the overtones of thy presence among us.

For those who are alone this morning and last night—
Alone in bars,
Alone watching television,
Eating alone in restaurants,

Lying alone in beds of pain,
Starving, alone—
We ask thy blessing.
Forgive our negligence,
Bind us close to Thee,
Then set us free, make us free.
Amen.

O God,

We thank you for Christmas Time,

And for all that it means to us.

We thank you that Jesus came into this world in a humble home;

We thank you that he had to grow up, and learn, like any other child;

We thank you that he did a good day's work, as a carpenter in a village shop in Nazareth;

We thank you that he was tempted and tired, hungry and sad, just as we are.

We thank you that he was one with us in all things;

That he shared our life, with its struggles and toils, its sorrows and joys.

We thank you for the service of his life,

For the love in his death,

For the power of his resurrection.

Grant, O God, that when he comes to us,

He may find room for him in our hearts,

For your love's sake.

Amen.

Complaint.
God of wisdom, our complaint this morning:
A malaise brought on,
The silent suffering of those in the neighborhood,
The stark, ugly face of hunger,
The turmoil of a world too quickly growing,
The imprisonment that makes us all jailbirds.

Appeal.
God of commitment, our appeal this morning:
Specific events of healing
For those with malaise,
For the physically ill.
Bring nourishment to the hungry,
And freedom to the prisoners.

Trust.
God of power, our trust is in you.
Some inkling of that trust has brought us together.
That trust encourages us to hear you in prayer, in preaching, and in praise.
Our trust, unshakably grounded in Jesus Christ.

Heavenly Father,
Who alone art good,
We lift up our hearts to Thee in this hour of praise and
thanksgiving.
We ask thy forgiveness:
For our lack of charity,
For our pride and self-indulgence,
For our self-worship,
For many words unfitly spoken,
For deeds done in spite,
For quarrels without purpose,
For a predilection for easy tasks—
Ones we can see and measure and finish, though we are called to
work at things more difficult—
For a certain lack of trust.
We ask forgiveness, in the strong name of Jesus Christ.

We pray thy healing:
Upon our own families,
Upon those whom we have met this week, who, of a sudden, are ill,
Upon those whose trouble is long standing,
Upon certain ones whose need is a pressure and a cause for worry,
Upon the very old and the very young, who are closer than we to
Thee,
Upon some whom we silently name in our hearts before Thee.
We pray thy healing.

We seek thy reconciliation:
Between neighbor and neighbor,

Parent and child,

Teacher and student,

Friend and friend,

Among the nations and powers,

Between the interests and wealth of the few and the dire need of the many,

For the divisions within, even, thy church—a cause of shame for the church—

We seek thy reconciliation, in the strong name of Jesus Christ.

These are our prayers: for forgiveness, for healing, for reconciliation.

We lay them before Thee.

Thy will be done!

Amen.

Dear God,

You invite us to an hour of reflection, thanksgiving, communion,
questioning, meditation, celebration.

Let us give thanks to the Lord!

This is a time to give thanks,

For food, for shelter, for health, for peace,

Which not all the world shares.

This is an hour for divine worship,

For remembering the saints of old,

For warming hands at the gospel fire,

For being still,

For keeping still,

For silence,

That, in the silence,

We might catch the faith of one who said:

The Lord is my light and my salvation—

Whom shall I fear?

The Lord is the stronghold of my life—

Of whom shall I be afraid?

Father,

We remember the Apostle said that, as a child,

He thought and spoke and acted as a child,

But that, in becoming a man, he gave up childish ways.

We know it is your will that we learn to live as adults and Christian men and women,

And to give up childish things and ways—

Yet fear of the future makes us prefer the familiar,

Even when that very common closeness hurts us.

This Advent season, we pray that we will grow into full adulthood, into the kinds of people you would have us be.

Give us the capacity for wonder,

The capacity for vulnerability,

The capacity to laugh at ourselves.

This season is wonderful, if we see the wonder.

But do we, Lord? Do we see wonder?

Or do we see a monotonous recurrence of things that have happened before and will surely happen again?

The coming of the Christ child to the humble manger in Bethlehem should, surely, give us courage to face the dark and poorer spots of our lives.

Does it?

Do we let ourselves be vulnerable?

Do we let ourselves be hurt for your sake, Lord?

Give us courage to be defeated in a good fight;

Give us courage to be beaten for a good cause.
Help us to be vulnerable for Thee, as was the babe in the manger.
Lord, if Thou has come to us—
If Thou has taken the burden of our humanity upon yourself—
If Thou hast come to us and brought us the salvation we could not give ourselves,
Then can we not be free to laugh at ourselves?
We pray to be given the gift of self-mockery,
So that we learn not to take ourselves too seriously.

This Advent season, we pray for the gifts
Of wonder, vulnerability, and self-mockery.

Dear Lord,
God of us all,
Source of life,
Our last and ultimate hope:
We lay before you the excesses of these last few days.
We stand alarmed, chastened, and humbled by excesses in spirit
and in body.
Some of us are awash in many hours of work;
Some are inundated by people and visits and parties and reunions;
Some see rolling billows of problems and worry, cresting ever higher
each day.

And, far away,
Others have cars under water;
Others walk past pools of blood in formerly friendly neighborhoods;
Others see homes covered in fire and ash.
"Eternal Father, strong to save,"[15]
Lift us above the small, nearby swells,
That we might help, in some small way,
To stem the surging tides of evil the world over.

15. "Eternal Father! strong to save" (1860) by William Whiting.

We come before Thee, the truth of the Living God,
With a week full of experiences—some good and some bad—
Remembering that Thou art a God who delights not in wickedness,
Who has no use for lust, gluttony, avarice, sloth, anger, envy, and
pride,
And so lets these things drop to the ground, dead.
We puff ourselves up—
You pop us like balloons.
We hide ourselves in half-truths—
You expose us as the dawn exposes the earth in the morning.
We are hard where we should be soft,
Soft where we should be hard.
Fearful! Fearful, in things large and small!
But Thou art the same Lord whose property is always to have
mercy,
And so, we enter thy house praying:
For healing for those who are ill,
For a sense of care, for a delight in giving,
For the will to discipline ourselves, to be taught by Thee,
In order to use all that has been given to us—
Money, television, telephone, automobile, food, clothes, shelter,
safety—
And not to be used by them.
We pray to do all to thy glory.
In this life, we know pain and confusion.
Lead us, Lord, for without Thee,
we are lost.

A thought:

There may be safety in the feeling of incompleteness or
uncertainty—

Otherwise, failure would give rise to the death struggle for success.

But this cloudier sense of "unrighteousness" keeps the ego off-
balance, alert, on its feet, asking questions of the speaker—

So, we are safe from triumphalism,

Safe from deadly certainty,

Alive to the Spirit,

Anxious for God.

A prayer:

We are not so smart.

We know that we can be broken, if asked to do too much.

We ask protection when the institutions that we have made—

Family, church, company, state—

When they turn on us and begin to eat us alive.

Give us a sure, sure sense of our ultimate worth in your eyes;

Make us wise as serpents, innocent as doves.

When we cry, "The night is dark, and I am far from home,"

Be to us a light in the dark.

O Lord, our God,
In Thee do we take refuge when the storms come upon us.
We shelter ourselves in Thee, for a time.
We shelter ourselves in thy faithfulness.
Heavenly Father!
Thou art our fortress and bulwark.
So many fears, like stray dogs, nip at us;
It seems as if we are torn apart by them.
A visitor—we are concerned.
The telephone—we are concerned.
A fire siren—we are frightened.
The daily mail—we are concerned.
The newspaper—we are concerned.
The hurt look in a loved one's eye—we are guilty.
Like a man running down a dark alley,
We are chased by the fear that surrounds us.
Lord God Almighty, save us!
Deliver us from the fear that pursues us.
We shelter ourselves in Thee.
Can we hear the words of thy Christ?
Will we, this day, hear and obey?
Will we, this day, trust and obey?
We shelter ourselves in Thee;
We wait in the cross's shadow.
Christ is risen!
Lord, hear our prayer.

Today, our prayer is for our country,
So troubled and hurt as she has been in the last week.
We pray for the healing of our countrymen, and others,
Injured in the fighting in Lebanon and Grenada.
We pray for the grieving families of those who died.
We pray that our own hearts will not harden against these deaths,
But that we have the grace to see each and every death as an infinite loss:
The loss of a child of God.
We pray for the many Christian and faithful people entrusted with the governance of this world.
In so many ways, our lives rest with their decisions and actions.
May our leaders be both strong and merciful;
May our citizens be both loyal and watchful;
May our wise hearts be both insightful, to know the truth,
And courageous, to speak the truth though it cost us dearly.
May our children be trained up in a way pleasing to Thee,
To prepare the way of the Christ and of his kingdom on earth.
May our senior citizens find ways to share their treasure of wisdom and experience with ignorant and naïve youth.
May our churches not shrink from the calling to be both in the world and yet not of the world.
Keep open our church doors to even the least of these, our

brethren.
May our Christian people once again hear the gospel call
To make each moment an act of worship.
Today, our prayer is for our country,
So troubled and hurt as she has been in the last week.
Lord, hear our prayer!
Amen.

God of our achievement and of our failure,

God of our kindness and of our bickering,

God of our insight and of our blindness,

God of our strength and of our weakness,

God of our honor and of our embarrassment,

God who is with us, in the springtime of well-being and in the autumn of discontent:

We are not at all worthy of Thee.

We skate on the surface of life when you would have us dive into its depth.

We do not notice that souls are being formed as the world hastens on its way.

Thank goodness for the Christ!

The Christ who helps us learn, in the simplest things in life, who we really are;

The Christ who gives us another day to learn the hard lesson of his love;

The Christ who moves like wind to make this world a better place;

The Christ who loves us, though we are utterly unworthy.

God of our sin and of our salvation,

God of our doubt and of our faith,

God of our friends and of our enemies:

Give us, this week, a closer walk with Thee.

In the powerful name of the Risen Jesus, we pray.

Amen.

The Bible questions us:
When the Son of Man comes, will he find faith on earth?
Adam, Adam, where are you?

"My God, my God, why have you forsaken me?"

"Where were you when I laid the foundation of the earth?
Who determined its measurements—surely you know!" [16]

Are you not one of them, Simon—one of the disciples of Jesus?
When the Son of Man comes, will he find faith on earth?
Let us all praise God.

16. Matt 27:46; Job 38:4–5, NRSV.

Almighty God,
Author of eternal life:
Illumine our hearts by the light of thy grace,
That our lips may show forth thy praise,
That our lives may bless Thee,
That our worship may glorify Thee.
Through Jesus Christ, our Lord,
Who taught us to pray together.

In this hour,
We will give thanks to the Lord with our whole heart.
We will tell of his wonderful deeds;
We will be glad and exult in him.
In this hour,
We will ask, again:
How shall we teach our children?
How does the heart grow?
In this hour,
We will give thanks.
Let us worship God.

Hear what comfortable words
Christ saith unto all that truly turn to him:
"Come to me, all you that are weary and are carrying heavy
burdens,
And I will give you rest."

Hear, also, the words of St. John:
"For God so loved the world that he gave his only Son,
So that everyone who believes in him may not perish
But may have eternal life."

Hear, also, the words of Scripture:
"The Lord is merciful and gracious,
Slow to anger and abounding in steadfast love."

"The sacrifice acceptable to God is a broken spirit;
A broken and contrite heart, O God,
You will not despise."[17]

---

17. Matt 11:28; John 3:16; Ps 103:8; Ps 51:17, NRSV.

Heavenly Father,
We ask for a sense of your spirit, this morning.
May our speaking and listening,
Our worship before you,
Be filled with marks of the truth that can set us free.

Heavenly Father,

What comfort it gives us again, to raise voices and hymns and praise to Thee!

Without Thee, our frustration would turn to bitterness.

Without Thee, our confusion would mean utter blindness.

Without Thee, our past would eat us alive.

Without Thee, we would have no reason to give, or to live.

It gives us comfort—

Though we stumble,

Though we straggle,

Though we sometimes think it might be more pleasant to forget the whole thing—

It gives us comfort to call on thy name,

On that name that charms our fears,

The name that sets the prisoner free.

Yes, it gives us comfort to raise voices, hymns, and prayers to Thee!

Amen.

Father,

In our prayers this morning,

We lift up the plight of the homeless ones on earth.

For those who, in Southeast Asia and Lebanon and the Bronx,
wander with no destination,

We ask that even our own far-off conduct might serve as a conduit
for their settlement.

With the very spirit of our own nation—

Which drifts, undisciplined—

We make a reckoning in our hearts.

For the homeless children near and far,

We ask a strong arm of support.

(How does each of us become a strong arm?)

For our own misdirection,

For our own homeless lack of hope,

We silently ask forgiveness.

God of Abraham and Isaac and Jacob,

God of the manger and cross and empty tomb,

God of the light that shines in the darkness,

Teach us that we are going home—

Lord, we tarry here awhile,

But we are going home.

Help us to understand the guidance in our Lord's Prayer

As, together, we invoke it.

Father,
We know that not a sparrow falls but that you know it.
We know that even the hairs on our heads are numbered.
We know that you watch over your children.
For your abiding care, we are thankful.

But we grieve, in this hour,
For one whose sudden death we did not foresee or expect.
We grieve for a loss that is permanent and painful,
And, down deep, we grieve for what might have been.
We hoped for more time.

Help us, in our remembering, to cherish all—in every life—
All that was solid and good and humble and Christian.
Help us to accept what has happened.
Chase from our minds that nagging and useless thought:
"If only . . .".
Bring us to a sound acceptance of death,
For we affirm the goodness in life,
We affirm care of all children,
We affirm reliance on Christ,
In life, in death, in life beyond death.

In this hour of grief,
Of memories, of acceptance, of strong affirmation,
We give our lives over, again, to this One we call Lord:
Jesus Christ.

Between the dark and the daylight,
When the night begins to lower,
The day's occupations pause
For a time that is known as the children's hour.

Father God, we pause now—
In the midst of the swirling weeks and months and years,
In the midst of the worries and sickness, the joys and sorrows,
The plain old hard work—
We pause, as children, to give thanks.

We give thanks for peace and prosperity, for comfort,
For a wide-open and rich land in which to live;
We give thanks for friends and neighbors,
For community and church.
But as we pause, between
The dark of our own limitations and failings
And the daylight of your Word,
We ask these things.

We would ask for your guidance,
As we work through the decisions that make our lives.
"Spirit of Life, in this New Dawn,
Give us the faith that follows on."[18]

We would ask your presence
With the physically sick and the emotionally distraught.

---

18. "Spirit of Life, in This New Dawn" (1928) by Earl Bowman Marlatt.

May they know the love of their neighbors,
And may their neighbors love them as you taught them to love.

We would ask your influence
On the great decision makers of our nation and world.
May they have the insight, energy, and creativity
So necessary in their trying situations.

Father God, we pause as children—
Your children—
Between the darkness and the daylight,
And ask your guidance in each and every one of our deeds.
In Christ's name, we pray.
Amen.

Heavenly Father—
You whom we do not know, cannot see, may not understand,
But who knows, sees, and understands us—
Why do the nations conspire?
Why do the peoples plot in vain?
Our rulers, all rulers, are set against us.
They do their own people great harm.
They trap us in great dark cities—
Detroit, New York, Caracas, Dar es Salaam, Hong Kong—
Chaining us with heat, ignorance, drugs,
With a great emptiness inside.
Our rulers have turned against the commandments of Jesus,
And we have let them get away with it.

Do we hear you laughing?
Deriding human pride that pretends to escape your judgment?
In fury, in proclamation, in faith, you have taught us to measure all
by the yardarms of the cross.
Lord, have mercy on us, thy disobedient children.
Have we not heard your warning to the rulers of this earth?
We have heard it.
Why, then, do we not echo it?
Have mercy!
Be wise!
Be warned!
Bow down!
Service justice with fear and trembling!
Our coming forward to pray rests on Christ Jesus.
We have heard of a king in a manger,

Surrounded with filth and commonness,
Raised among us—the measure of all things.
You said to him, "You are my son; today I have begotten you."
Praise to Thee, O Most High.
In Jesus' name, we pray.[19]

19. Ps 2, NRSV.

Heavenly Father,
How great is thy name, O Lord our God, through all the earth!
To mention it brings us peace.
We fall so short of thy purpose for us, though,
That we ask special blessings:
Deliver us, we pray, from evil.
Close our ears—
To gossip,
To false teachings,
To the raucous din of television,
To the selfish requests of our inner hearts,
To the counsel of fear and timidity—
That we might hear no evil.
Close our eyes—
To backward glances that do no good,
To fascination with others' wrong,
To our own minor good,
To the approval or disapproval of men,
To blank stares of material finery—
That we might see no evil.
Close our mouths—
To character assassination,
To unnecessary criticism,
To rough language,
To thoughtless, thoughtless words,
To flattery—
That we might speak no evil.
Heavenly Father,
How great is thy name, in all the earth!

Wood on wood,
The rocker rubs the floor.
In a haze of pipe smoke,
The spaniel whines.
He dreams,
His master muses,
The rocker rolls and creaks.
A hundred pictures, a thousand memories—
"To sleep—to sleep, perchance to dream."[20]
The rocker repeats its cadence of peace.
Hearth, and heart,
Red in crackling amusement.
Wood on wood,
The rocker remembers.

20. *Hamlet* (1602) by William Shakespeare.

Lord who restores us,
In you we do not long for the wrong things,
For you mock us when we do.
You force us to stop and rest,
When we would rather lay ourselves to waste with striving.
You take us by the hand alongside still waters:
There, we see our own reflection in the pool.
We lean over the lake
And peer at our own image—
My!
What a sight!

Lord who restores us,
You do not desert us, nor do you leave us alone
To be devoured by our own presence.
You drag us along,
Prodding us to live worthy lives,
For your name's sake.

Lord who restores us,
We trust you in dark corners—
Not because we feel confident
(Heaven knows how we fear, and fear, and fear),
Not because we deserve your comfort
(We are undeserving, much as this appalls us).
We trust only because we take you "at your word."

Lord who restores us,
We scent the aroma of a great banquet,
Prepared for those who hunger and wait.
And we are quieted,
And we are quieted,
And we are quieted,
And we are touched,
And we are—restored!
Christ is risen!
He is risen indeed!
Surely, goodness and mercy shall follow us all the days of our common life,
And we shall dwell in the house of the Lord, forever.

Index